The She-Wolf
of Tsla-a-Wat

The She-Wolf of Tsla-a-Wat

Indian Stories
for the Young

Anne Simeon

Illustrations by
Douglas Tait

Douglas W. C. Tait

J.J. Douglas Ltd. Vancouver

For all the young Modeste Henrys
of the Khowutzun Indian Reserve

J.J. Douglas Ltd.
1875 Welch Street
North Vancouver, British Columbia

Canadian Cataloguing in Publication Data

Simeon, Anne, 1911-
    The she-wolf of Tsla-a-wat

    ISBN 0-88894-145-5

    1. Indians of North America - Legends - Juvenile literature. 2. Indians of North America - Northwest coast of North America - Legends - Juvenile literature. I. Title.
E98.F6S54   j398.2'097   C77-002143-3

Design by Nancy Legue
Typesetting by Domino-Link Word and Data Processing
Printed and bound in Canada by Hunter Rose

CONTENTS

Introduction:
Before and After
the White Man Came

*P*retend you are living on the northwest coast of North
America before the white people came. Of course you are
an Indian.

You cannot imagine life without the sea. When a storm is
blowing, the waves thunder up the long sloping beach where you
live. They almost reach to the great houses and tall totem poles
set around the bay, and the spruce, hemlocks and cedars at the
edge of the dense forest behind your village are salty with spray.
On calm days the waves roll lazily. Then you can have fun in
the small dugout canoes and tickle purple starfish clinging to
the rocks.

Your home is built of cedar planks with whole tree trunks
for posts and beams. The house is enormous—big enough for
most of your clan, which is made up of uncles, aunts, first
cousins, second cousins, third cousins and cousins so far removed
that it takes you a long time to learn how they fit into the
family. But learn you must, for relatives, and especially
ancestors, are very important people. A Wolf, Bear, or some
other animal is painted on your house front. This is your family
crest. It is shared by everyone in your home because you all
have the same ancestor who founded your family and who, you
believe, once took the form of your crest animal.

You call your home a *thee laylum* if you belong to the Coast
Salish tribe. It means Big House in your language.

Your *thee laylum* may be a hundred feet long or more, but it
has only one room. At one end a large corner is reserved for
your clan chief, and along the walls each family has a living
space of its own. The families are usually separated from one

1

another by cedar bark mats or by stacked painted wooden storage boxes or woven baskets.

Your bed is a bench raised a little off the floor and the mattress is made of bulrushes. Your mother has spent many long evenings weaving blankets for the family, using cedar bark which she has pounded soft with a flat bone hammer. She has woven in with the bark mountain goat hair, hair from your little white dogs, feathers, duck down and other materials from animals and plants. Your father must have traded with tribes living farther inland for the mountain goat wool. In exchange he gave them things they needed from the coast such as whale oil, dried halibut, or dentalium shells which they used for money.

The baby in the family is rocked to sleep in a wooden cradle hung from a pole. You may have helped gather bundles of a special kind of soft moss for the baby's diapers.

If you are a girl you help your mother cook on a fire burning on the dirt floor between your family space and that of the family living opposite you. There is no chimney, but most of the smoke escapes through holes in the roof.

At night the *thee laylum* is lit by the fires and by candles made by floating wicks in clam shells filled with whale or seal oil. The oily little oolichan fish make good candles when they are dried.

During winter evenings the Big House can be a magical place filled with the exciting sound of drums, clacking rattles, singing and the thud of bare dancing feet on the smooth dirt floor. This is when guests are being entertained at a feast which can last for many days. Plays are performed by actors wearing fantastic costumes and masks representing monsters, animals or birds such as a huge raven with a long snapping beak. Special family masks, crests and other important possessions are shown for the visitors to admire. Stories are told of brave deeds and strange happenings. Gifts are exchanged, games played and ancestors remembered in songs and dances.

Extra-delicious food is brought in enormous wooden dishes carved in the shape of a canoe, animal or bird. Great decorated horn or wooden ladles are used to serve the food, and everyone sits on the floor to eat.

The dishes are placed on cedar bark cloths. In homes where place mats of fern are used, the cloths stay clean for a long time. You use clam shells and mussel shells for spoons as well as for bowls. There are cedar bark napkins for people who like to take food out of a dish with their fingers.

Your favorite food is probably salmon and shellfish. Then come duck soup, and cakes made with berries and seaweed mashed together with fish oil and pressed into wooden moulds to dry. Dog salmon hearts threaded on sticks and barbecued are good, too. Winter is the time for you to enjoy stews of meat from deer, elk, bear and other animals the men have hunted in the forest.

Winter is also a good time for storytelling. It is a favorite occupation for the old people whose eyes are not good enough for carving or weaving in the dim flickering light of the Big House. Some of the tales are funny and some are sad. Some tell the history of your tribe. Some teach respect for animals, and the spirits of the sea and forest who can harm or protect you, depending on how you treat them. Many of the stories teach lessons on good behavior. You become very red-faced if the lesson tells about your broken promise, disobedience, rudeness to an elder or some other misdeed you have just been guilty of. Being shamed in front of your relatives is probably your worst punishment. You never get spanked.

There are no schools, but you have many lessons to learn from your elders. After the age of seven, boys are taught by an uncle, girls by an aunt.

There is so much to learn because everything you use, eat or wear comes from material found in nature. For instance, how is a giant cedar cut down with only stone hammers and stone or wooden wedges? How is a dugout canoe made which is big enough to carry forty warriors on a raiding expedition? Or an eight-man canoe strong enough to go far out to sea in search of a whale, or buck stormy weather to attend a feast on a distant island? How is flour made out of fern roots? What about paint? How is a spruce root basket woven tightly enough to hold water? How do you make string out of nettle fiber? harpoon points out of elk antlers? arrowheads out of stone? knives out of mussel shells? What must the hunter know about the ways of the animals and the fisherman about the ways of the salmon? How did the world begin? What were the adventures of your ancestors? You have to learn the answers to these questions and many more.

Boys are trained to be tough and brave. It is hard not to shiver after a swim in freezing weather, especially when your uncle is waiting to beat your back and shoulders with fir branches until the blood runs. And not to whimper when you are beaten, even when stinging urine is rubbed into the wounds. This is a daily lesson.

Even babies must learn to control their crying. Mothers pinch their noses and hold a hand over their mouths at the first sign of a wail because the lives of brothers and sisters may one day depend on silence. A war party from an enemy tribe may raid your village. The big war canoes creep silently along the coast at night. Houses are attacked when everyone is asleep. Many people are killed with clubs and spears. Others are taken away for slaves. If a lookout has been able to give warning of the raid, the women and children run to hide in the forest. It is scary crouching among the rustling trees in the dark, listening to the sounds of fighting close by and hardly daring to breathe for fear of being discovered. This is when a child must somehow manage not to cry or make a sound.

A girl's training is not so hard as a boy's, but there is plenty to learn in preparation for looking after a family of your own. One day you will make their clothing out of animal skins, cedar bark, and fur. You will gather berries and nourishing roots in baskets you have woven, and will dry and store food for the winter. Sewing, cooking, weaving and preparing hides are only some of the skills a girl is taught, for, like your brothers, you must learn to manage a canoe well enough to beach it in surf without getting wet.

Only part of the day is taken up with lessons. There is time to play with small bows and arrows, and balls made of tightly rolled deer hair covered with hide. Big boys enjoy darts and sports like wrestling and tug-of-war. And you have contests to see who is best at throwing a spear through a rolling hoop, or shooting at targets with an arrow. This is good practice for when you become a hunter. Shinny is a popular game to play on a long sandy beach, and guessing games with painted sticks and pebbles are fun.

One day you will spend a long time alone in the forest searching for your guardian spirit whose supernatural power will always help you. The spirit may be in the form of an animal you will meet in an unusual way, perhaps in a dream.

Strange pale men with blue eyes, yellow hair and bushy beards may come to your village from the sea in great objects which are not canoes although they move through the water. They will speak a strange language in loud voices. They will try to hand you brightly colored beads. The grown-ups in your village will not be singing welcome songs as they usually do when friendly visitors arrive.

You may be scared and hide in your *thee laylum* until the strange men have gone away.

Perhaps you will be the first child to see a white man on the northwest coast.

Gradually life will change as more white strangers come bringing surprising and novel things such as iron tools, mirrors and guns. Your people will give sea otter, bear and beaver fur in exchange. Some families will move from the villages to live near the white men's settlements where they can barter furs, carvings, and baskets at the trading posts. These people will be the first to abandon the Big Houses and to sample the white man's food, which they will find easier to prepare than the berries, roots and shellfish they have gathered and cooked in the traditional way. Your mother may enjoy bartering spruce root baskets for saucepans and bright cotton material to replace her cedar bark skirt. In time few native housewives will remember the old ways of clothing and feeding their families.

The changing life may seem good to some people, but to most it will be confusing, and worrying, too. Missionaries will come to your village urging you to worship their God who, they say, is more powerful than your spirits—even your guardian spirit. Listening to your elders' conversation you will learn that too many white men are coming to your country and pushing your people onto small Reserves. You will hear about alcohol which makes men crazy, and smallpox, the terrible sickness which kills, and which your medicine man cannot cure.

The elders will also speak angrily about the white man's laws which punish your people for holding gift-giving feasts and dancing in their ceremonial dress and crested masks. You will be puzzled when you hear that your warriors have been ordered to stop raiding expeditions: you will wonder how else slaves can be captured and wrongs righted. Later you will hear of children being taken away to schools where they must learn the white man's ways, and being spanked when they speak their own language.

More changes will come as surely as the curling wave rolls up your beach. Your great-great-great-grandchildren will ask, "What were the old ways of our people?" Some of the answers will be found only in books.

The stories in this book were first told in a dimly lit *thee laylum*. The storyteller imitated a baby's whimper, the swoosh of an eagle's wing, a grandmother's lament. And his face took on the terrifying scowl of a cannibal giant. Books cannot do that. But the stories are written here in a way that hopefully all children—white as well as Indian—can enjoy.

The She-wolf of Tsla-a-wat

*L*ong long ago an Indian band belonging to the Wolf clan lived on the shores of Tsla-a-wat, an inlet close by Vancouver. Now the inlet is called Indian Arm.

This band was very proud of its family crest of a Wolf. It was carved on the house posts and it decorated many of the wooden dishes, tools and other things used by the people.

The story of the Wolf was a favorite one among the Tsla-a-wat children. Grandparents never got tired of telling how the village was once deserted and left in ruins and then, many years later, it was again filled with happy people. And all because of an inquisitive Mother Wolf.

The children were told that a terrible sickness came to the village in that long ago time. Everyone died—all except one tiny baby boy. He was too young even to have a name so we will call him No-name. There was no one left to care for him and he would have died too if a she-wolf had not come by and, seeing no people about, started sniffing around the village. She wondered where everybody was. It was so quiet. No sounds of children playing or men busy at their work. There were only the calling of gulls and the grating *Krrkk Krrkk* of two ravens wheeling high in the sky. The tide was far out, but no one dug clams on the beach. No smoke curled from the blackened smoke holes of any of the buildings.

The she-wolf nosed around till she was satisfied that no harm threatened her. Then she trotted into the house where No-name was sleeping. She padded about, sniffing at the dried meat and fish hanging from the roof beams. She spent some time gnawing a deer bone which was lying in the cold ashes of a fireplace. Then, licking her lips, she wandered up to the baby's cradle and peered in.

The she-wolf gave a little whine of surprise when she saw the baby, whose black hair was sticking up in wisps around his head. When No-name woke up and began to whimper, she was reminded of her four cubs she had left in their den on the hillside.

She gazed with steady yellow eyes at the tiny face, so hairless, which grew all puckered up as the whimper turned into a frightened wail. As she gazed, she sniffed. This must be a man-cub, she decided, recognizing the same scent she caught from hunters in the forest. But where was his mother? The she-wolf hesitated. Surely this small thing must be cared for, and just as surely there was no one here to care for him. Quickly she made up her mind. She took the baby up in her powerful jaws and started for home.

On her way through the fir forest the she-wolf had to put the child down several times and have a rest. She carried him gently, but it was hard to hold his squirming little naked body. As for No-name, being carried in a wolf's mouth was a very strange and scary experience. He was used to being carried on his mother's back. Also, he missed his warm cedar bark blanket and his diaper of soft moss.

8

The she-wolf . . . wandered up to the baby's cradle.

The wolf cubs were whining with hunger when their mother arrived at the den. She lay down and stretched out her long shaggy body so that the little ones could suck her milk. She knew that the man-cub must be hungry too, and cold, so she put out a paw and drew him close to her soft warm belly where he sucked greedily along with the cubs.

Babies' memories are short. The little orphan quickly forgot his wooden cradle. He even stopped wondering where his mother was. Cuddling up to his woolly foster brothers and sisters, he soon felt as if the den had always been his home, and the wolves his family.

After a while No-name and the cubs ate food which the mother and father wolf had chewed up to make soft. When some teeth had grown they learned to eat mice and little rabbits. Then came the time for hunting lessons. Of course No-name could never hope to kill the animals the cubs were being taught to stalk, but he shared in the lessons and did the best he could.

The child grew big and strong on the raw red meat of deer and elk. Having never tasted the food that humans eat, he did not miss it. Nor did he miss the joy of playing, for wolf cubs enjoy games of tag, hide-and-go-seek, and wrestling as much as any boy. The she-wolf and her mate treated No-name as their own and were very proud of the son who walked on two legs and had no fur on his body.

One day, when No-name was a teenager, he went exploring by himself. After wandering for some time in the forest, he came to the village where he had been born. In amazement he stared at the great empty houses, now falling into ruin. Surely these were dens. But who had lived in them? Certainly not wolves. Inquisitively, No-name examined stone tools and weatherworn wooden dishes half-hidden in the long grass. What could these strange things be? While still puzzling, No-name noticed a bow and arrow. They were lying in the shelter of a big rock which had saved them from spoiling during the many years of sun and rain.

No-name picked up the bow and arrow. After fiddling with them for a few minutes he saw how they could be used. Before long he sent an arrow flying straight and true to hit the tree he aimed at. No-name could hardly wait to get home and show his exciting find to the family. Next day, when hunting with his foster brothers, he killed a deer with his arrow. The wolves were astonished, and prouder of him than ever.

Although happy enough, No-name did sometimes wish he could find someone like himself. He realized that he would some day be man—perhaps he had some faint remembrance of his father. But where did his own people live? The wish to find them grew stronger and stronger. At last No-name decided that he must go away and search for men. He sat beside his foster mother and stroked her soft gray fur, trying to make her understand what he had to do. He promised that she would be remembered forever among his people, if he could find them.

So No-name set out on a long journey which took him far across the mountains to the rolling plains. One day he stopped at the top of a low hill and looked down onto a large group of strange, cone-shaped objects. Soon people appeared and No-name realized that the objects were dens lived in by humans like himself. He ran as fast as he could down the hillside toward the tipis, for that is what the cone-shaped objects were.

The Plains people welcomed the young stranger, offered him a home, and promised to show him the ways of men. Before long No-name married a pretty young girl from the tribe. When he told her about the beautiful country he had come from, with its great forests and mountains and the bountiful sea, she agreed to return there with him. After many weeks of travel they arrived at the shores of Tsla-a-wat.

The young husband and wife had lots of children and their children had more children and so on down the years until once again the village was filled with busy, happy people. No-name kept his promise to his foster mother by making a Wolf the proud crest of the clan that he founded.

The children of the Wolf clan loved this story about their ancestor. They never shivered at the thought of wolves as some children do. In their hearts they loved them because if it had not been for that she-wolf, no one would be sitting in a Tsla-a-wat lodge listening to the tales of long ago.

The Waskos:
Dogs of the Sea

A brother and sister once lived on the Queen Charlotte Islands, at a place called Hunter's Point. There was a beautiful beach there, with rocks and pools and plenty of sand. Close by, a group of fir trees shaded a grassy spot where it was always cool on a summer day.

One afternoon, while Brother and Sister were digging for clams, they heard a funny noise coming from this group of trees. It sounded like a puppy whining for its supper. In fact it sounded like two puppies whining for their supper. At first Brother and Sister thought that some of their little white dogs had followed them and were in trouble.

"No, it sounds like baby animals," said Brother. The children peered among the trees and, in the hollow of a rotten trunk, found two furry brown puppies.

"Oh, aren't they adorable!" exclaimed Sister, stroking the soft fur and silky pointed ears. "However can they have got here?"

"Let's take them home and keep them as pets," said Brother.

"We'd better ask Father first," objected Sister. She was the elder, and rather bossy.

So Brother and Sister ran to their father, who was carving a feast bowl outside their house.

"We've found some dear little puppies in a tree. Can we

bring them home?" gasped the children, quite out of breath from running up a steep trail from the beach.

They led their father to the hollow tree trunk. When he saw the two cute little furry faces, he promised his children to raise the puppies as pets.

How those puppies grew! In no time they were enormous, quite as big as wolves. And they looked like wolves, too. But they were so playful and gentle that the children were not scared of them, although the very thought of real wolves made them shiver.

The children's father chose a name for the dogs. He gave the same name to both of them—Wasko, which means Dog of the Sea. He had a strong feeling that the animals had a special power, a sort of sea magic, which would be of help to the tribe.

And they had, as you will find out.

One day, when the Indian people at Hunter's Point were short of food, the two Waskos ran into the sea and started to swim, using their strong front legs as paddles. Sadly Brother and Sister watched their pets swim right out of sight.

"They'll be drowned," sobbed Sister.

"They'll never come back," cried Brother. Even their father became a little nervous, but again he had the feeling that the Waskos would bring good to the tribe.

The Waskos did return a few hours later.

But what a surprise!

Each one was carrying not one whale, which would be astonishing enough, but three whales.

How could it be possible? You know the size of a whale.

In the hollow of a rotten trunk they found two furry brown puppies.

It is far, far bigger than the most enormous wolf. Yet with the help of its magic power each Wasko had a whale in its mouth, another between its ears, and another on its back. The one on its back was held by the Wasko's curling tail.

Every morning the great dogs swam out to sea. They brought back so many whales that soon there was hardly room to walk on the beach. Everyone in the village was busy from morning to night, cutting up the huge animals with mussel-shell knives, feasting, and storing the good food for the winter.

The boys in the village had to gather wood and bark, and help to keep the fires going. All day long cedar wood stewing pots bubbled and steamed as hot stones were thrown in to keep the water boiling while it cooked the whale meat. Other pots, suspended over slow fires, melted down the fat to take out the oil, and racks of meat roasted beside red embers. Special kinds of smoky fires had to be watched in the smoke houses where strips of meat were hung to dry so that they would keep for a long time.

The young girls helped their mothers store the cooked food in cedar boxes and they poured the whale oil into skin bags, or into the bulbous part of kelp. There was work to do for weeks. Even the whales' backbones were scraped and polished so they could be used in the lodge as stools for important guests. As for the little children, they scooted about, getting in the way, and holding out sticky brown hands for the lumps of whale blubber which were so good to chew on.

All the work was very tiring. Brother's and Sister's mother thought of a good way to take a holiday and get away from the sight of whale meat for a while. She decided to pack some up and take it to her mother, who lived in the village at Skidegate. Her husband thought it would be nice to get away, too, and of course Brother and Sister went along with their parents. The Waskos were left behind because they were clumsy dogs in a canoe. "Please don't catch any more whales while we are away," pleaded the exhausted family as they said good-bye to their pets.

The family had to spend a long time at Skidegate because of a storm. Brother and Sister should have had a lovely visit with their Grandma, but unfortunately she was not at all nice. For instance, once when there was not enough food for everyone she refused to share her store of delicious salmon eggs. Also she was always annoying the children's father. She should not have returned to Hunter's Point with the family, but she did. And all because of her a very sad thing happened to the Waskos.

As soon as everyone was home Grandma did something to annoy the father again. He was so angry that he decided to punish her.

Now, Grandma's favorite supper was a dish of limpets and mussels soaked in fish oil. She spent a long time gathering the seafood and her old back became terribly sore from stooping, so that she was glad to sit down to prepare her feast.

As soon as he saw Grandma settled with her dish, the children's father sent Brother to fetch some whale grease which had spilled on the beach long ago. It was now bad and smelled horrible. Brother brought the nasty stuff back in a clam shell and, when Grandma was not looking, his father quickly poured it over her food. She had no idea what was happening until her mouth was full of the rancid grease.

It was awful!

How could she ever get rid of the dreadful taste?

Her supper was completely ruined—after all that trouble!

Grandma was furious. Who can blame her? Brother and Sister could not help laughing when they saw the old woman's face all puckered up with disgust and anger. They were unkind to laugh at the trick played on an elder, even if she did deserve it.

But Grandma had her revenge.

Early next morning she noticed that the Waskos had gone whale hunting again. She made a fire by the sea's edge, heated some stones, then put them in a pot which she had filled with sea water. When the water was boiling she poured it back into the sea.

Grandma had mixed some bad magic in the pot and immediately the sea became so rough that it was doubtful if the Waskos could swim safely home. Grandma knew how much the family loved their pets, who had by now learned to bring in whales only when they were needed. And she knew that the whole tribe was enjoying whale meat and oil without the hard work and danger of hunting the great animals themselves. "If the Waskos never came back," thought Grandma, "it would be a good revenge for the insult I received."

Brother, Sister and their father were very upset when they realized what had happened. They looked out to sea.

Grandma was furious. Her supper was completely ruined.

Neither Wasko was in sight, only the angry, tumbling waves.

"Let's go up onto the cliff so we can see farther," suggested the father. All three scrambled up the rocky cliffside and looked out at the boiling sea again. Suddenly Brother shouted "I can see them!" Yes, the Waskos were struggling through the rough water, trying to reach the shore. The beach was near, but the dogs were thrown back by the waves every time they tried to reach it.

They turned and battled their way to a headland called Lawn Hill Point. Here at last the Waskos were able to clamber ashore. Exhausted, they dragged themselves up the sloping beach, flopped down onto the warm sand, and fell into a deep sleep. By the time their family reached them the Waskos had turned into two beautiful silvery rocks.

Perhaps you will visit Lawn Hill Point some day. If you do you will see the two rocks still there, lying side by side on the sand. You will say, "There lie the Waskos, Dogs of the Sea."

20

Marooned
on Gitrhahla Island

*C*hief Girtrawn ruled the Salmon Eater tribe, who lived near the mouth of the Nass River, on the northwest Pacific coast.

It was a good place to live because there was so much food easily available. One summer there was far more than the Indian people could eat. The men had to make new cedar wood boxes in which to store dried food for the winter, and thin wisps of smoke curled out of cracks in the smoke houses day and night. But still there was a lot of fish, meat and other good things left over.

"Let's send a gift of smoked salmon, dried berries and oolichan oil to my old father on the Queen Charlotte Islands," suggested the Chief's wife.

This was a good idea, but who could take the food far across the sea to the Islands? Chief Girtrawn had to stay home to look after his people and most of the men were away hunting the seal.

"Let me go," said Quawm.

"Me too," said Kilaeskiles.

Quawm and Kilaeskiles were the Chief's sons. They were young and already were good paddlers of the family's dugout canoes, but they had never been on a long trip by themselves. Their mother was doubtful about letting them go, but their father said, "It is time our sons learned to do

21

the work of young men. Let them take an older companion and we will wish them well."

The boys were very excited at the thought of their journey. Happily they helped their mother load one of the best canoes. They put in stacks of dried salmon, boxes full of sun-dried berries and seal bladder bags of seal oil. Then they took up the paddles and prepared to set off. With them was a young woman who had been chosen to see that all went well with the boys.

The mother had a last word for her children:

"Mind you make straight for the Queen Charlotte Islands," she called to them. "Don't stop anywhere or some bad thing may happen to you. Even if you see a nice sandy beach, do not go there to play."

"We will do as you say," chorused the boys.

They meant it at the time.

But long before they got to the Queen Charlotte Islands they passed close to Gitrhahla Island, which had the most beautiful beach Quawm and Kilaeskiles had ever seen. They simply could not resist taking a closer look at it. And having paddled to the shore they could not resist running the canoe onto the shining sand and jumping out.

The young woman who was supposed to look after the boys forgot to remind them of their promise. In fact she was only too glad to get out of the canoe and stretch her cramped legs.

It was a wonderful beach. There were satiny logs to jump on, and shallow pools full of curious darting sea animals. The sand was soft and fine and warm for bare feet to run on, yet cool and firm where the sea had lapped upon it.

Quawm and Kilaeskiles were so happy playing on this beautiful beach that they did not realize how late it was getting. Nor did their companion, who had spent the whole time sleeping in the sun. When the sun went in she did not wake and no one noticed the big, black clouds in the sky until a rain drop bounced on the young woman's nose. And patter, patter—splashes of rain began to make tiny dents in the sand.

It was the beginning of a storm.

Everyone ran for shelter under a big log. They thought the storm would soon be over. But the wind started to blow and it rained harder than ever, as if it would never stop.

Suddenly Quawm remembered something. "The canoe!" he shouted. "It will be full of water."

Quawm, Kilaeskiles and the young woman ran through the driving rain to the water's edge. Horrified they stared at what had once been a very fine canoe. Now it was full of water; but even worse than that, a long split showed in its side where the wind had pushed it against a jagged rock. Worst of all, their precious food was ruined in the salt water. Only a few drops of oil had been saved because the seal bladder bags had burst when the canoe hit the rock. The boxes of berries were smashed and the berries were at the bottom of the sea.

Not only was there nothing left for Grandfather, there was nothing left for Quawm, Kilaeskiles or the young woman either. Only a couple of salmon fillets were fit to eat.

The split canoe was useless. Together the boys and their companion bailed out the water and pulled it farther up the beach. Then they turned it over and crept underneath to get out of the pouring rain.

They were wet and unhappy, and hungry. "We should have listened to our mother," said Quawm sadly as he shared out the last few pieces of smoked salmon. "Yes, she said a bad thing might happen if we stopped anywhere," sighed Kilaeskiles. "We'll never get off this island now," moaned the young woman. All three began to cry softly.

The cold rain poured down for six days. All that time Quawm, Kilaeskiles and their companion lay under the upturned canoe, too cold, miserable and hungry to do anything else. There really was not much they could do. The boys had neither weapons nor tools because they were not old enough to hunt or to repair a canoe. As for the young woman, she was a very silly person and no help at all. Who knows why the three of them did not gather mussels from the rocks, or edible seaweed from the shore, but for some reason they did not.

On the seventh day Quawm, hearing footsteps, peeped from their shelter. He saw a strange-looking man wrapped in a long black cloak. At once Quawm had a feeling that the man was a Spirit.

Quawm was right. He was looking at the Eagle Spirit of the Sea in human form.

"Oh Spirit," said Quawm in a voice weak from hunger, "we were going to the Queen Charlottes with a gift of food for my Grandfather, but there was a storm and our canoe split and we are starving."

24

His shining black wings were yards long, and so was his tail.

By this time the others had dragged themselves out from under the canoe, almost too weak to stand. The stranger looked at them for a long time; then at last he said, "I will help you."

He stretched out his left arm and immediately it sprouted black feathers and turned into an enormous eagle's wing. With it he scooped up the astonished young woman. Almost before they knew what was happening, Quawm and Kilaeskiles were tucked under the right arm, which had sprouted wing feathers too.

"Hold tight," ordered the Eagle Spirit, "and don't look down or an accident might happen." Then he rose swiftly into the air.

None of the Eagle's passengers had the slightest wish to peek, for they knew how scary it would be to see the gray ocean far below them. They all clung tightly to the Eagle's body under his wings. The feathers there were soft and warm and the journey would not have been too bad if the swish and swoosh of the powerful wings had not nearly deafened everybody as they thrust through the air.

Swooping and soaring with great speed, the Eagle Spirit flew straight to the Queen Charlotte Islands, where he landed at a place called Gilkayo.

"Close your eyes and don't look till I am gone," he said. This was because he did not want to be seen in his true Eagle Spirit form. The boys covered their eyes, but the young woman could not control her curiosity. She opened her eyes and saw the supernatural bird in all his glory. His shining black wings were yards long, and so was his tail. He had long white feathers on his head and neck. A black feathery cloak covered his powerful shoulders.

"Just look at that immense bird," exclaimed the young woman. As she spoke he dived into the sea with a tremendous splash which shook the trees and rocks for miles around and scared the boys and their companion almost out of their wits. Fearfully they watched the great bird sink slowly under the sea, as if he were drowning. Forgetting that a Spirit could come to no harm, they sang a mournful song, then set out to find Grandfather's village.

Instead of receiving a welcome gift of food, Grandfather had to give his hungry visitors what little he had. This made Quawm and Kilaeskiles feel terribly ashamed. Shame is a very bad feeling for Indians and was an even greater punishment than being marooned for six days on an island in a storm.

Later in the year Chief Girtrawn took the Eagle Spirit of the Sea as his family crest, in gratitude for his sons' rescue.

Every time the boys saw the crest they were reminded that it is always best to obey the elders.

Littleboy-halibut

At Naden Harbour, on the west coast of the Queen Charlotte Islands, there is a rock which was once a spirit called Chief Rock. One day, enraged by some insulting visitors, Chief Rock ordered a slave to block the harbor and so prevent them from leaving. The visitors were lucky to escape by another route. The slave was a gigantic and evil Crab.

He was so big that his long pinching claws stretched all the way across Naden Harbour. He was so big and fierce that even the great killer whales went out of their way to avoid him. He was so big and fierce that he scared the salmon away from the coast so that the Indian people had to go without their favorite food. And none of the bands dared to build a village at Naden Harbour, which is a pity because it is a very beautiful place.

Some people belonging to the Eagle clan lived a little farther away, at a place called Dawson Harbour. They were scared that the Crab might go to live near their village. "Who knows how long we may remain safe," warned the old chief. "Let us take our women and the little ones and all our belongings, and build a village far away."

So all the people packed up their possessions and set off in their canoes. But one old lady refused to leave the place which had always been her home. She begged her little grandson to stay in the village with her and, because he loved his Grandma, he agreed to do what she asked. The boy's name is not known, so he will just be called Littleboy.

When everyone else had left Dawson Harbour, Littleboy had no one to play with. But he was quite happy to spend all day on the beach with driftwood and shells for toys, and the sea gulls for friends.

Grandma often complained that there was no one now to hunt for meat in the forest, or to bring home a fish; Littleboy was too young and his grandmother too old. It is true there was plenty to eat, but Littleboy and Grandma soon got tired of the sweet berries and plants they gathered from the forest. Even the mussels and seaweed found on the beach hardly satisfied them. They never stopped longing for the good taste of fish.

One day, when Littleboy was amusing himself tickling purple starfish in a pool, he heard a whirring sound above him. He looked up to the sky and saw a huge Eagle holding something in its claws. The Eagle was so big that Littleboy knew it must be the Eagle Spirit of his clan. As he watched, something dropped, landing a few feet from Littleboy. He ran to pick it up.

It was a fine, medium-sized halibut.

"A fish! The good Eagle Spirit has brought us a fish!" shouted Littleboy as he ran up the beach to tell his grandmother the good news.

She was delighted to know that at last they would have a good fish supper. Quickly she took a knife and prepared to cut off the halibut's head and tail. But before she could start, the trees in the forest began to sway violently as if a

He put the halibut skin on himself, like a cloak.

great wind were blowing. The rocks on the shore trembled and shook, making a loud grinding sound. And the calm sea suddenly rose up into a huge curling wave. It looked as if it were about to sweep right over the beach.

Grandma at once threw down her knife.

"This fine fish is telling me not to cut its head and tail off," she said. "Maybe I will be allowed just to skin it." As soon as she had spoken the trees became still, the rocks stopped their trembling, and the curling wave rolled back into the sea.

So Grandma very gently skinned the halibut. She put the meat aside to roast later by the fire, then hung the skin, complete with its head and tail, on a branch to dry in the warm sun.

A few days later Littleboy noticed that the halibut skin had dried. He took it in his hands and then a very strange feeling came over him. Almost before he knew what he was doing he had put it on himself, like a cloak. The skin had a magic power which made it stretch till it fitted Littleboy perfectly.

"I'm a halibut, I'm a halibut boy!" cried Littleboy excitedly. He ran down to the sea and dived in. He could not wait to see what it felt like to be a fish.

What a fine swimmer Littleboy was now. He swam under the water for hours and hours. He did not have to come up for air and he did not get tired at all. He was just like a fish. Littleboy-halibut swam all around the world and back again.

Grandma, who had been very lonely all by herself, was so glad when at last her grandson came home. She was

31

happily listening to his stories of all the wonderful things he had seen in the world when they heard a loud voice saying, "Now you are full of magic power; go and kill the terrible Crab at Naden Harbour." Littleboy knew that the voice came from a spirit because there was no one to be seen. Obviously, the Crab was still scaring away every living thing that came near his sea house.

Littleboy gladly dressed himself again in the powerful halibut skin. Telling his grandmother he would soon return to her, he ran back into the sea and quickly swam along the coast. He soon reached the entrance to Naden Harbour. Sure enough, it was blocked by the Crab's monstrous body. It squatted at the bottom of the sea with its great back to Littleboy-halibut. Silently he crept along the sea floor toward it.

Littleboy-halibut started to chew the beast from behind. The Crab was so huge that it could not turn around. It could do nothing to save itself from being chewed up, claws, shell and all. Soon there was nothing left of the cruel monster.

Of course such an enormous meal in his stomach made Littleboy-halibut feel very sick. So he threw up the chewed pieces of shell and flesh, saying, "May these turn into harmless small crabs for people to enjoy eating forever."

And the pieces did turn into little crabs as soon as they touched the bottom of the sea. In no time hundreds of tiny crabs were scuttling about here, there and everywhere.

And ever since, crabs have been a delicious food for all the people who soon went to live at beautiful Naden Harbour, and all the other places by the sea.

Four Brothers
and a Cannibal Giant

Na-wa-ka-wie was an Indian chief who lived on the west coast of Canada long ago. He had four sons.

Na-wa-ka-wie taught his sons to be brave and to fear no one—no one, that is, but the savage cannibal giant who lived in a valley on the far side of a mountain ridge behind their village. "That is the Forbidden Valley," the Chief was constantly warning the boys. "Never let me catch you venturing even to the top of our ridge. No bow and arrow, no spear, no club will protect you against Baxba-kwa-nux-sie-wie, the Fierce One."

While they were still very young the boys were only too glad to obey their father. But as they grew older they began to think that they need not heed the old Chief's warning.

"Even if we did meet the monster, surely the four of us would be a match for him."

"Let's beg our father to let us at least hunt mountain goat on the ridge so we can look at the Forbidden Valley."

The brothers would often talk in this way together and at last their father allowed them to hunt on top of the ridge. But they had to promise not to go down the other side into the giant's territory.

Happily the boys took up their bows and arrows and set off. Na-wa-ka-wie called the eldest one back, saying,

"Tawik, my son, take these four magic articles which you must use if you find yourselves in danger, as I fear you may." The magic articles were a comb, a skin container of fish oil, a black stone, and a twist of black goat's hair.

The boys eagerly scrambled up the mountain. From the top they gazed in wonder at the beautiful valley below them. A river which looked like melted silver wound through green, flower-studded fields. Over all lay a thin, weaving mist with streaks of red swirling through it. Looking closer, the boys saw that this curious mist was rising from pretty, small houses clustered along the river bank. Standing apart from the main group was a very large dwelling which had a thick column of blood-red smoke pouring through the smoke hole. Tawik knew that this house must belong to Baxba-kwa-nux-sie-wie, the Fierce One.

There was no one to be seen about the village, and the Forbidden Valley did not look forbidding at all. It looked positively inviting in the bright sunshine which gleamed through the mist.

In his excitement at seeing this beautiful new country Tawik forgot the mountain goats, his father's warnings and even the promises made. He felt he simply must explore the valley, and started down the mountain. At first his younger brothers held back, but Tawik pointed out that obviously the villagers were away hunting. And in any case, he added, had not they decided that four boys as strong as they would be a match for the cannibal, should they meet him?

When the boys reached the house with the red smoke

they peered through the open doorway. At first all they could see in the dark room was a small log fire burning on the hearth. Then they noticed a fat, ugly old woman and a young boy sitting by the fire.

When the old woman saw the strangers she motioned them to a log bench and silently watched as they sat down. The eldest brother began to feel uncomfortable when he noticed that the boy was staring at him and fidgeting nervously. When he asked the old woman why her son was staring, she pointed to a trickle of blood oozing down Tawik's leg where he had scratched it on a thorn bush. "My son sees blood on your leg and wants to drink it. . ." But before she had finished speaking the boy had thrown himself down on the dirt floor beside Tawik and was greedily licking his blood.

Tawik began to feel less brave when the old woman stoked the fire and got out a gigantic cauldron. He decided that only a trick could save the boys from being cooked for Baxba-kwa-nux-sie-wie's dinner. He took up his bow and shot an arrow through the open doorway, calmly asking his youngest brother to fetch it for him. The boy willingly ran from the house and set off for home. The old woman became suspicious when Tawik shot off two more arrows, telling his other brothers to bring them back, but he assured her that he was only practising his skill. Then he shot a fourth arrow and, politely excusing himself, he followed it and ran for his life.

When Tawik did not return, the old woman shuffled out of her house and called to her husband, who was working in the fields. "Our good dinner has run away," she

He struggled through the branches, the sharp thorns holding him back . . .

screamed, shaking her fists at the retreating figures. The giant threw down his tools and took off after the boys. By this time Tawik had caught up with his brothers. He could hear Baxba-kwa-nux-sie-wie lumbering after them with gigantic strides and was terrified that they would be overtaken. Suddenly he remembered the four magic articles his father had given him. The time had come to use them.

He took from his pocket the magic comb and hastily stuck it into the ground behind him. Immediately a thick clump of closely knit brambles sprang up and the boys widened the distance from their pursuer as he struggled through the clinging branches, the sharp thorns holding him back as they tore at his clothes.

But soon the gap narrowed again and as the giant drew near, Tawik threw the magic black stone over his shoulder. It instantly changed into a high cliff. Baxba-kwa-nux-sie-wie was forced to claw his way up, his great clumsy fingers clutching at the smooth rock face for handholds.

Rage gave extra speed to his long legs. He was almost onto the boys again when Tawik threw the third magic article, the skin container of fish oil. As the thick liquid poured out it quickly formed into a lake which the giant had to flounder through as best he could.

The brothers sped on, but they were still a mile from home when they felt a hot, panting breath close behind them. Quickly Tawik tossed the magic twist of goat's hair into the air. It opened out and formed a dense fog. Blinded, cursing and choking, Baxba-kwa-nux-sie-wie had to struggle through the swirling cloud—but all was clear ahead and the brothers gained distance again.

At last their home was in sight. With a burst of speed they eluded a pair of huge grabbing hands and crashed through the door of their house. They slammed it shut and barred it. But the boys were not yet safe. Throwing his great weight against the house, the giant threatened to break it to pieces. And he would have succeeded if Na-wa-ka-wie had not called out, "Fierce One, come again in four days' time and you shall have two of my juiciest sons to eat."

The giant, who was tired after the exhausting chase, agreed and ambled off, grumbling.

The Chief decided that his sons had been punished enough for their disobedience. In any case he would never dream of handing over any of them to the cannibal. He decided to get rid of Baxba-kwa-nux-sie-wie for good. Just as Tawik used a trick to escape from the old woman, so Na-wa-ka-wie used a trick to overcome the giant's savage strength.

He ordered his slaves to dig a deep pit at the side of his fireplace. When finished, the pit was hidden by an old couch which had no legs. The front of the couch rested on the floor, but the back, supported by props, overhung the pit which was covered with cedar boughs.

The trap was ready when the giant returned, bringing with him his wife and son. The Chief received his visitors with the usual courtesy. He seated them in the place of honor, on the couch, and told them that a feast was being prepared. Afterward, he promised, he would hand over two of his juiciest sons. The giant family was pleased with all this attention. Their mouths watered at the thought of the feast, to be followed by a fine dessert of human flesh.

Na-wa-ka-wie entertained his unwelcome guests with long, dull stories. His droning voice, the heat of the fire, and a magic sleeping song hummed by slaves in the background soon sent the visitors to sleep. Their rumbling snores were a signal for the slaves to knock the props from under the back of the couch. It overturned and threw the sleepers into the pit. The slaves threw hot rocks and scalding water over the struggling giant family, killing them all.

Next day Na-wa-ka-wie burned the bones and scattered the ashes in the wind, saying, "Baxba-kwa-nux-sie-wie, Fierce One, thou shalt pursue men for all time and never know rest." This was meant to be an eternal punishment in the land where the cannibal's spirit would go.

But Baxba-kwa-nux-sie-wie had his revenge. His ashes turned into mosquitoes, black flies, no-see-ums, and all other kinds of stinging insects which have been a nuisance to mankind ever since.

Quamichan,
the Flying Cannibal Giantess

*I*n the long ago days a wicked flying giantess named
Quamichan lived on Saltspring Island. The swoosh of
her great wings was like the blowing of a winter gale and
the sea rose up in foamy waves whenever she passed over
it. At her approach the fishermen took up their cedar bark
bailers and prepared to save their canoes from being
swamped. Then they prayed for the safety of their families
on shore.

Quamichan often flew from her home on Saltspring
Island to Khowutzun Bay (on maps it is called Cowichan
Bay). She liked Khowutzun Bay because many Indian
families lived there. She liked the Indian families because
they had many children. And Quamichan liked children
very much because they were so sweet and tender.

Quamichan was a cannibal giantess, which is the most
scary kind of all. And children were her favorite food.

None of the boys and girls at Khowutzun Bay felt safe.
They never knew when the giantess might swoop down on
them as they played outside the lodges or went clamming
on the beach. And they hardly dared to paddle the small
canoes out into the bay to jig for fish because there would
be no time to scurry for safety when Quamichan came
flying. She would dive down, grab a child in her huge
clawing hands, and stuff him into a basket made of live

Quamichan was a cannibal giantess . . . children were her favorite food.

snakes twined together in a squirming, hissing mass. Then she would fly home across the sea to Saltspring Island.

Quamichan always chose the plumpest children and, for a special treat, cuddly babies.

One day the giantess decided to give a feast at Khowutzun Bay. She had to spend a whole week stealing children from all over because so many people were invited to the party. One by one she bundled boys and girls and cuddly babies into her dreadful basket and took them to a nearby dark and scary mountain cave.

At first the bigger children looked for a way of escape from their prison. But it was no use. The cave had been hollowed out of the mountain, which rose straight from the rocky shore far below. There was nothing to do but huddle together and pray to the spirits for help, while the little girls stifled their sobs as they comforted the wailing babies.

When the cave was filled with children, Quamichan set to work digging an enormous pit down on the beach. At the bottom of the pit she placed large flat rocks. Then she shuffled into the forest for giant armloads of bone-dry twigs which she piled on top of the rocks. Next she heaped on fir boughs and great chunks of bark. Quamichan happily twirled her firestick until sparks began to catch the kindling. A few puffs from her powerful lungs and the sticks began to crackle and spit as tongues of flame flickered up into the pile of wood.

Quamichan intended to roast the children as soon as the rocks became red hot.

Now she fetched the boys and girls and cuddly babies from the cave. She sat them around the fire, which was already hot enough to singe their hair. The poor little things sobbed and begged to be taken home, but Quamichan did not hear them. She was dancing about with excitement at the thought of her feast: "What a good meal we will have," she chanted. "How good these human animals will taste, yum, yum." Her great wings were flapping and fanning the fire to make the flames leap ever higher, and her voice was nearly as loud as thunder.

Every minute the rocks in the pit were getting hotter and hotter. Soon they would split apart and begin to glow red. They were almost ready to roast the children when the first guest arrived. It was Quamichan's sister. She was a kind woman who felt sad at the sight of the sobbing children. She decided to save their lives and get rid of her cannibal sister for good.

"Dear Quamichan," she said in a wheedling voice, "you sing and dance so beautifully. I wish you would dance around the fire once more so I can have the pleasure of watching you."

Quamichan was vain. She was only too happy to show off her dancing skill. While leaping about she did not notice her sister pick up a long stick which was lying on the ground. She did not see it placed across her path as she danced. She tripped over the stick and, with a loud yell, fell on her back into the flaming pit. Quamichan screamed, "Pull me out! Save me!" But her sister and the children gathered up sticks and threw them on the fire so that it blazed up even more fiercely than ever.

In a few minutes the flying cannibal giantess was dead.

Giant sparks floated up into the air, where they turned

into herons, ducks, robins, and every other kind of bird. They swooped around in the sky until only a few ashes were left in the pit, then flew off to make their homes in Khowutzun Bay and all over the country. Some of the birds built their nests in the forest bordering a nearby lake. It has been called Quamichan Lake ever since.

As for the boys and girls, they hugged the cannibal's sister and shouted "Hych ka See am," which means a great big "Thank You" in the Khowutzun language. Then the children from Saltspring jumped into canoes and paddled across the sea to their island, singing as they went. And the Khowutzun Bay children scampered back to their village, carrying the babies with them.